THE MAN WHO SAWS US IN HALF

Southern Messenger Poets

DAVE SMITH, SERIES EDITOR

THE MAN WHO SAWS US IN HALF

⋗ POEMS ⋚

RON HOUCHIN

[signature] Ron Houchin
Sissy
2018

LOUISIANA STATE
UNIVERSITY PRESS
BATON ROUGE

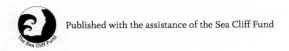

Published with the assistance of the Sea Cliff Fund

Published by Louisiana State University Press
Copyright © 2013 by Ron Houchin
All rights reserved
Manufactured in the United States of America
LSU Press Paperback Original
First printing

DESIGNER: Michelle A. Neustrom
TYPEFACES: Whitman and Brothers
PRINTER AND BINDER: IBT Global

LIBRARY OF CONGRESS CATALOGING-IN-PUBLICATION DATA

Houchin, Ron.
  [Poems. Selections]
  The man who saws us in half : poems / Ron Houchin.
    pages cm. — (Southern Messenger Poets)
  "LSU Press Paperback Original"—T.p. verso.
  ISBN 978-0-8071-5111-2 (paper : alk. paper) — ISBN 978-0-8071-5112-9 (pdf) —
ISBN 978-0-8071-5113-6 (epub) — ISBN 978-0-8071-5114-3 (mobi)
  I. Title.
  PR6058.O77M36 2014
  821'.914—dc23
                                                    2012048525

Grateful acknowledgment is due the editors of the following journals, periodicals, and other venues
where some of these poems first appeared, sometimes in earlier versions: *ABZ*: "The Intentions of Trees";
Birmingham Poetry Review: "Measuring the Moon"; *Five Points*: "Séance"; *Nantahala Review*: "Visible Songs
of Appalachia"; *New Mexico Poetry Review*: "Frozen Light"; *Poetry Ireland Review*: "January Night Testament,"
"Summer Tenants," and "The Man Who Saws Us in Half"; *Still*: "In Mythic Times" and "River Night";
The Stinging Fly: "Between"; *Valparaiso Poetry Review*: "Hymn to Her"; *We All Live Downstream* (anthology):
"In My Town" and "My Father's House."

The author wishes to thank Director Mike Mullins and the teachers and staff of the Appalachian Writers'
Workshop, Hindman Settlement School, Hindman, Kentucky; and Darnell Arnoult, Silas House, Marianne
Worthington, Dave Smith, and Kathryn Stripling Byer for their encouragement over the years.

For my grandson,
Griffin Alexander McCormick

⤙ CONTENTS ⤚

THE MAN WHO SAWS US IN HALF

January Night Testament

I was born in a new year but
with an old sense of the contrariness
of things, the resistance of snow to
darkness, the reluctance of shadow
in light, the distant tapping on hardwoods,
the owl singing its one-syllable lullaby.

Even that old expanse, poorly lighted,
from house to barn that I got used to
gave opportunities—each time I put
the horses up—for tripping
on blown-down limbs along the way.

In the barn, among cold hay and
manure, with never enough
light to see pitchforks lying about,
rakes parked out of stall, or saddles
I was to uncinch—just the familiar
body heat and breath of Gray

and Celia showing my hands the path,
as if the only thing about our
intentions that can't be thwarted is
the memory of purpose, like the space
between winter trees not even
the woodpecker can destroy.

So Tired

The lord of the playground hangs
exhausted as rusted nails,
his elbows crooked around
pipes of the jungle bars.

He wonders whether his friends have left,
his followers have forsaken him.
Three crows land above his head hungry
for the falling light of his eyes.

The blood cannot drip from his cracked nose;
failure penetrates each cell.
In this lull of play, sun disappears;

leaves, like saints, forgive; wind, like a demon,
tries turning over an unloaded bus.
So tired, to raise his head, open his eyes
would be like parting waves.

What is worth looking up to?
Heat blisters,
light blinds, and birds, like dreams, always
come back to ground.

If the world had been the aura
he saw between slides and swings then this
were no defeat.

But every bit of light
is glare, signs and hours posted, distance
around the track, prohibition of bicycles
and glass containers.

He's left to think,
and hang near the flagpole while last crows
search the images he thought were play,
when play was the world.

The Green Snake

My hand and forearm imitate
and magnify him when I paint
on the copper jewels of his eyes,
the black makeup of thin stripes.

I see his hunger in my fingers'
straightening and nails' parting
to swallow the young frog I have
molded out of river clay.

Tonight when I follow him up
from the creek to block his path,
to tread upon his tail, I lose him
in the grass behind the well—

My arm wriggles along the blades
and stretches to bite the moon
because I cannot shape
his need to slip away.

Summer Tenants

The white spider riding
my shoulder from the reed bush,
like a bit of cotton down,
will not be here long enough

to get to know. The sweat bee
that mines the wet crease
of my neck had hummed through
the door, disoriented as a vacationer
dropping his bag in the vestibule.

From late spring, the neighborhood might
as well be Ireland, Egypt, or Patagonia,
full of creatures that come with "Ninety
Days" stamped on their passports.

I don't begrudge them their itineraries,
any more than I do their lives, but
the speed at which they buzz over
my perennials, looking only
at what drew them from the brochure.

Interpretation of Silence

You cannot find silence in the morning.
A wall cracks, the house settles
into its chair of earth. You wake,
yawn deafening, jaw popping.
Carolina wrens shout in trees out back.

Even in the stillest moment, breath saws
your nose.

When you finally start to rise,
make coffee, all that sings holds
an E through the first swallow.

By noon, it's impossible to hear silence
under the hectoring sun.

Alone in the racket of traffic and dread
toward home, you hold dinnertime's illusion
of quiet between bites—the symphonies
of spoon and fork at least are short.

Afterwards, you escape into the yard
for the air between maples. When
you were the child among leaves,
soundlessness was the negative space
around words.

Finally, there is no finally. The sun shuts
up and there's the cranky lamp
of the moon, the static of close stars—
a hint and a reminder of intimacy.

Tomorrow, waking from islets of dream,
you have illusions of beginning to hear again.

Katherine Skating the Ohio, 1916

Late December, everything brown
or buried under a pall of snow,
a girl with only the fore-hope of family

and grandchildren waits without muff or mittens
beside the narrow river, among other young
of her small town, as the great wagon

is pulled cross-river testing the strength of ice.
When the all-clear bell clangs from the other side,
with river transformed to thickest glass,

she pushes out, above lunker bass
and phantom catfish, to cross and re-cross
the Ohio like the Shawnee of her past.

Her borrowed blades scraping, etching similar
circular forms, for no other reason
than joy of motion in a stopped time—

images from family history, in the only picture
between wool cloud and lace snow I have of her,
grandmother so young and alone, in my head.

String Theory

There is no deep reality, just phenomena.
—NIELS BOHR

I loved to untie the tense knots
of leather laces,
to have each strand lying before

me unwound like the secret
watch that hides
the heart spring of the game I kept

looking for, no matter how round-
about and clumsily,
taking extra breaks for iced tea

or Kool-Aid, coming
back from rain and the tic-tac-toe
of wide puddles,

scissor cut of fun, the over-the-shoulder
memory of stop, catch,
and throw, until the day after all

seasons leave town, the sun's
back up and I run out with restrung
glove to first base.

Reverence for Beds

Because the blankets are peeled
back across pillows, pulled aside like lapels,
because I fall back on the cushions at the death
of day, fatigue growing

its cancer, because my hands
fold in imitation of cherubs, and I face
the ceiling like a corpse, because the future is
coming one blink at a time,

and I feel myself fading
between sighs, I lie in state beside
the nightlight's moon-glow with windows
and shadows at hand.

Regal in my gown.
Aftershave, toothpaste taste in my mouth.
The after-hours air of a dark house, because I
dream now

the first scent of rust, the well
bucket and mold-taste settling in water, the surprise
of a little hide and hair in the sausage, heaviness
in the biscuit, splinter

from the churn, old world flavor
of each dream, because I fall like Icarus flown
too close to the moon; wings frozen, I land face-
down on covers, back into day.

The Good Earth

In 1955, I think it may be good,
but every other minute I change
my mind. Rolling downhill
after my Hopalong Cassidy
cap gun, the unknown hand
of tree root knocking the flesh
from my left knee, I swear
screams of certainty the earth
is evil, a trap for us who come
to summer backyards to play.

Time tells conflicting tales
about pain. Mine is horrible
but Larry, Moe, and Curly's fun.
I cannot side yet with Einstein
or Pearl Buck about benevolence.

But then I see my torn knee,
bones that move me by changing
angles, muscles that push, pull,
as Mrs. Boylan, from next door,
so quick, leaning over me
with iodine, bandage, and scent
of Coppertone, in her white bikini,
blows the sting away.

River Night

They bob out here reminding
each other that none of them
knows what they are, the little boats

that glow in land fog rolling down
from hills—very rare. Late
river tide rises, opening air

in vapor. This is not nature alone,
but the Corps of Engineers. Barges
bang each other barking

like rust-colored dogs in the city
pound. Upriver, the lock-and-dam
sifts every bicycle part, bit of Styrofoam

cooler, barbecue grill, and aluminum
foil that tangle and grind in its baleen
teeth, and cannot look away.

Body Farm

(At the University of Tennessee
hundreds of dead people lie in a field
for the forensic study of bodily decomposition.)

In the meadow their bones crumble
like saltines pecked by birds.

Some hug clumps of grass like pillows;
others snuggle under black plastic or pose

in bowers of tangled brush and wind, yet more
lie like nudists nonchalant in the openness

of seasons. All are visited often in summer
by fireflies swooning on widening reek

or by slaps of thunder. Where schools
of earthworms, wave on wave, swim beneath them,

they wait to freeze in the fingerprints of snow
or under glimpses of starlight on clear nights.

I suspect a kind of peace when their heads
finally break down, from loosening rain

and absorbing earth, in a slow
re-enactment of the war between states.

Lament of the Retired Coal Mine Canary

(i.m. Kathy Miller)

If I could learn to be a bird again,
not just for the lofty view from lost mountains
or windy top limbs of gone oaks, but to sing,
the air in my lungs like feathers lifting me.

If I could learn to dance on wire and wing
to see the world that I need to see,
but I have breathed, below, through
flash fire, coal dust, and smoke.

If I could still be a bird, I'd thread myself
cloud to cloud. From my window cage
I watch the day, mouth open like a fish.
The serious bellows of my chest no longer enough,

my air comes pinching through blackened
nostrils, and I have left in my head
only the breathless echo of each tunnel.

Tending the Fire

When I'd gathered more oak and ash than
needed for the night,
my purpose changed to making use
of the good wood I should not waste.

I sat on one log staring at the moon like a book.
Fire applauded endless stars;
kindling stretched and cracked its joints.

Light took communion with air for the fifty
trillionth time.
And I was there, just ashore,
surrounded by Earth's hasty little ships.

Glass and Water

Be glad that you have come.

—INSCRIPTION, 1ST CENTURY A.D.
ROMAN DRINKING GLASS

In the museum, light, visible and invisible,
through Ennion glass, searches
for its other self.

At home, the everyday glass and water,
half full or half empty, light up
like lovers in each other.

Always before, drifting, unborn as sand
and water flesh, they waited. Tonight,
the stare of March stars

chills an empty glass on my sill,
and water that's worked its way
here from the same

everywhere, forms from an icicle,
like a votive seed, falling
from eaves to glass bottom.

The Coal Globe

It sits by my grandmother's black Bible
on her bedside table with the water glass

that holds her uppers. I sneak in,
having night sweats and insomnia at eleven,

to hear the soft flutter of her breath.
She seems harmless, asleep

beside the glass-trapped scene of a small town
where wagons wait at mud curbs,

and miners hold their buckets under sooty arms
before "Old Logan," mine No. 37.

A black sun locks up the sky. I crouch
in the L-shape of her bed and table,

as if under a protecting arm. Like a small
dream caught in a larger one,

the baseball-sized orb glitters, coal dust
lifting, when I shake it. Sun is sifted

in the narrow street. Again miners' faces
feel light. Horses turn warm brown,

the mineshaft shrinks before bright rays.
What looked like dull hydrants scattered

on walkways become children waiting for fathers
and uncles. Everything's clean, free,

for the second. Then motes begin landing
again, to re-freeze the day under black snow.

Tender

Tender is the knife,
whereas the revolver
is boisterous,

rapping knuckles,
cracking heads,
slapping its

friends' hands
too hard each
time they meet.

Remember me,
says the knife,
sleek, magical, silent

in the hand, each lover
smiling back
like a scar.

In Praise of Comb-Overs

Those acts of antigravity
afforded by applied layers
        of hairspray

are not just living paradoxes,
but things of beauty,
elaborate daily pageants,
        defying descent:

The Shell's a lacquered wave along the part;
The Forward Sweep splits into
Alfalfa bangs swept hard
right and left; the Forward Foldback
doubles the hair back on top
        creating a hairline
        to die for—all are fine.

But it's the Las Vegas Swirl of L. A. Roy,
the mesmerist, that denies all logic
and invention, wrapped around
his head like a silver turban
taking five cans of Sudden Beauty
        to maintain balance
        and sheen. Where's
        the romance in shiny pates,

plugs, or transplants? With mullet websites
abounding, why not create one coffee table book
of comb-overs, from Taj Mahal-overs to Tumbleweed-overs?

Oh, I love the bowled-over,
yet demure, presence of a pseudo-pompadour.
I would stand and applaud the auteur under his work

for the illusion of full stoppage
of time, well
coiffed, wind
the only nemesis.

Lost in the Cemetery

Less than twelve, I count graves where some
letters are gone as if fallen into grass.

First time out of the car, among stones
that bear short stories, "Beloved Son,"
"Devoted wife," I walk by the markers

that line up like apartments.
Thinking of the dates as addresses, I fear
some might sleep through my stick tapping

on their door, my reading of their names
aloud. I wonder whether they are always
at home and if that is what it means to be here.

I rub across lichens, test the firmness
of roots, kneel among mayapples—
their light green out of place.

Under a kudzu fence, I listen to the breeze
through tangles, as if vines, too, hear my calling,
and know where the lost might be.

Stray City Dog

I always imagine his life—
treading up greasy
and proverbial
from the viaduct,
between Salvation
and Karma,
knowing everyone by what
is held out, seeing
each gesture as
offering—to be holy.

My Father's House

My father's house stands far back, where
no evening or morning breeze of memory stirs,
as far back as a dream of Logan County,

West Virginia where folks sit at tables and stand
beside chairs in bald gullies and stripped terraces,
as if my father's house were sucked up into air

by a tornado that lifted the heavy and left the light.
All the places where he and I would've lived
are torn open. Nothing—neither parking garage

nor vacant lot—remains where strange cars
or chewing cows could wait and wander, places
where we might have grown up and older

across from each other's morning cereal bowls
and coffee mugs. In my father's house, I am
the one who walks between walls and falls

through floors looking for a stair to climb, a bed
to raise dreams in, a closet to hang shirts and pants,
a tree to stand under. In my father's house

where he forgot how to breathe, where I have
still to live, we look out at the ghosts
of mountains that used to be our homes.

Everything Is a Place

Having sat long on the red table by the door,
the white urn has province; its neighbors,
the parlor palm and the black umbrella stand,
get to know it. Their molecules begin to mix.
This bright vase received ambassadors
from the yellow wall. Then you came back
after six weeks, lifted and wiped it, placing it
under the counter, holidays of grief commencing
in the hall. To these things you're despot
from the blue, alien abductor in their world.
The whole house hears of your offense.
Things want to be right again. You think
it craziness? Well, the day you left, I returned
the urn to its place where it blushes in the sun,
and around it peasant dust sparkles. Reverence
for the places of things offers a kind of peace.
We celebrate your long comet's passing.

Why I Watch the National Geographic Channel

It used to be for the naked
native bodies, the family
of the flesh, the clarity
of never deciding what
to wear. But nowadays

it's to see Uncle Rory
in the slouching
orangutan. To find what
I recall of Aunt Betty
in the red of the baboon.

To have that sympathy I always
wanted for Mom and Dad
stoking fire outside their hut.
To hear the wolf's howl
hollow out the night

sixty thousand years ago.
Or to see myself in the dinosaur-
dodging mammal and have
the oldest sense of family known.

Snails in the Garden

There, they're their own best hope,
on the littoral
overlap of rock
    and soil, tiny grunting
    archaeologists,
each lugging
    a large knapsack
of tools home from
    the day's dig.

Mermaid's Funeral

When my cousin Charlotte drowns,
they close the lid, lowering the coffin
like a submarine. I watch her drift off

in her narrow boat to live under
an ocean of grass. I spy her
from my sleep, another kind of sea,

where she arranges shells and cups,
setting up her floating dolls, her teddy bears
for tea that won't stay in the pot.

She ventures lonely out to play and swims
up to the roof of her garden house to walk
the edge like a sleepy acrobat. I wake

to scribble notes in the garden, leaving
letters under rocks and invitations
in trees. Since she won't be back

for birthdays, I dig a hole for her
candled cake. She lifts her mask
of leaves and makes a wish with rain.

At the Casto Sleep Clinic, 1995

Watching myself sleep
automatically makes it a dream,
even on video tape.

Like an infant fading,
my body begins relinquishing
itself back to space.

Watching my ribs let go
in rhythms of dream, I attend the little
funeral between breaths,

a fly landing
on swatter wires to scent decay and begin
the hold on good-bye.

Reflections of the Shape Shifter

Like a noun suggesting action
      but gradual,
he bent to pick up cola cans.
      He could
be a park bench for three or four seconds.
      His long coat, colored
like tent canvas starched by lightning
and soaked in night, helped him
shift
      to whatever was near.
In an alley, head down
      he shopped,
a hound in rubbish.
I'd spy him from the bus on my way
to town.
      Fascination began once
as I glimpsed him in a window near dusk.
When I passed on my bicycle
      that evening, a shapeless
      lump blocking
      light in front
      of the hardware store
      caught the corner of my eye:
one hand, like a paw,
      guarded a match's flare against
evening river breeze. As fire neared his face
and touched the tip of his snipe,
      he sucked in flame.
      I saw features bright as baby flesh,
even in the dark window,
      a dust of freckles
across the nose,
      and deep blue eyes.

In the gaps of an unevenly buttoned
shirt,
long breasts hung,
each with its broad pink nipple.
  It was late and sight could not
be trusted. I pumped hard
  all the way home,
  a peddle broke
off as I flew into the yard.

Hidden Places That Open Suddenly

She leapt out of the barrier phlox—
her nest tucked in the weed cluster
near the creek. When she lunged

at me, my ball cap could not keep up
with my head. She skittered into bridge
center leading me as far from her

young as she could. Catbird-clever,
she jumped on the guardrail
then dropped over the side.

I had to follow her disappearance
into water or bridge underbelly
to let her know I did not want

to bite into her fledglings' lives.
Then I did not go home to suss-out
from Audubon which avian nation

was hers. Now I remember
her as guide into the flushed
heart of everything.

The Intention of Trees

After the lumberjacks left, I sawed
with my small flashlight through the hills
of stumps arranged in lightning.

A will of roots still gripped ground,
though wishes for tall futures left air.
Their pantomime of night at noon will

no longer shade our cars. Broken limbs
penetrate and sparkle in dark rain as if leaking
the desire to hold earth and sky apart.

I wonder whether lumberjacks were named
for Jack the Giant Killer. With intense bright
blades toward wood, axe men found the one

mechanism that holds the world in place.
Soon gods will butt heads in many storms
over our understanding. I pick up one

of the last leaves and hear elegies of wind.
Remaining chords still ring.
Felled branches point like duty to the sky.

Thin Quarters

Not these federal coins
of copper and alloy,
but the old silver disks
with edges like teeth;

I carried each one long
enough for George to lose
some hair. I kept them because
I was poor and their magic did

not thin with age like men.
Such quarters melted down might
still ward off evil. Instead
of the fifty states where

the new ones pretend
to belong, the old ones were
from Philly, Denver, or Frisco,
depending on the strike.

Swaggering into Gladwell's
Pharmacy to count sodas
and adventures I could buy
with John Carter of Mars

or Tarzan of the Apes, I wished
for handfuls of thin quarters
that could simply saw
through every pocket I had.

One Step Removed

a ghost of a ghost . . .

—JIM MINICK

If ghost is the body one step
removed, like the wavy lights

reflecting on the river,
the ghost of the ghost's a memory,

and the ghost of recollection,
a dream. Most nights when I go

down to water's edge in sleep,
moonlight lies heavy on my shoulders

and my hand shines when I lift it,
much like yours on mine

when we walked here in wet grass.
Again, the moon carves our shadows.

Made You Look

Each untruth I construct forms a simulacrum I love,
like puppet or scarecrow—dark eyes open,
allowing no seeing inside.

I look down his hollow gullet to the clutter
of his chest to other fabrications throbbing there.
Spiders crawl about tying everything up

in shriveled web. This is my brother
in similes of uncertainty, metaphors of doubt
I claim him only as doppelgänger. There's no air,

not a single word from him, just pantomimes
to distract. See, here his hand rises.
His lids flutter. Try not to look where he points.

The Man Who Saws Us in Half

1.

To see his Chinese lanterns and his sleight of hand,
we hang on fences or crouch in garage windows
when he practices in his backyard.

Walking our attention around his fence, he holds
it aloft, like a medicine ball. When the sun
rises, high overhead, he draws a dark cone up to hover

over his worktable. He swirls his wand under
its shadow until lightlessness dissolves
like cotton candy.

He practices on rainy days by floating
eight red umbrellas over his work.
We see no wires.

2.

Pointing and bowing, he ushers each of us
into his long box. I remember him
smoothing the pillow for my jerky head.

He lowers the lid with a double click. I lie
there lost, watching him
lift the shining blade. The wood rasps

its long monotone. He saws then pulls
the box in two, wheeling both parts
about his yard. Now, at a distance,

I see my Redball Jets and wiggle my feet
without trying. After hauling the halves back
together, he lifts me from the rejoined box

and rolls it through the backdoor where
we are forbidden to follow. I stand
but cannot take a step without looking down.

Luuletaja

(Estonian for *liar* and *poet*)

When you tell me I should not lie,
Mother, I don't know where
my mind should go, like what to do
with my hands at a funeral.

At Uncle Ivor's service in the Tallinn
Funeral Home, I had to go
so badly I couldn't keep my hands
from my pockets. You gave me

the dirty look and I crept out
to the toilet. When I returned,
the director had closed the coffin
and ushered everyone out to the carts.

But I never got to say good-bye, so
I lifted the lid, shook Ivor's hand,
and mussed his hair the way he did
mine so often. You believe that, don't you?

Frozen Light

I wake in the middle of a clang, the clock glowing 4:16 A.M.
Dream sighs, smells of cold-damp hang like winterberries.
Nothing stirs. No one is awake.

Something's in the barn disturbing the new harvester.
Pulling on the thickest Christmas socks I ever received,
I think, *What can anything do to such a hard machine?*
Go back to sleep. But I know I won't.

A light is on under the snow and the moon's the size
of a washtub that only early January produces. As I tread
to the barn in loose boots, the ironies begin to untrim
the tree of my mind: It is night, but bright

enough to show the wide door of this livestock enclosure
I've padlocked to house an appliance. My hundred Herefords
scatter through hilly pastures; I fret for a new device as if it could
shiver. Stars take hold of the pull rope of morning.

Oscar, our tabby, is silhouetted in the loft, chomping the barn rat
he chased all autumn. His whiskers twinkle in false dawn.
I stand squarely in the center of everything that I love.

The Lost Rhetoric of Memory

(for Cathy Smith Bowers)

Each hour the memory of those already gone
pads over to stretch out beside me,
like a panther. Then their names come after,
a litter of new kittens.

Mother, Lonnie, Charles . . .
—all different sizes but the same age,
like the uniformity of wordless loss.

Each time I try to put phrases to their going,
it feels coarse, like shirts made from scraps,
or the biscuits children bake

in toy ovens—facsimiles smelling of salt,
but full of lumps, raw dough,
and thicker than my throat.

The Sudden Mind

When I was young, deer
leapt the deadfall
behind me and I spent
my dogs charging after.

But years have let decay
of towns surround the wild,
and I squander the day
hunting a wastrel squirrel.

No matter how much I hound
rotting logs, stiff brambles,
and dry clusters of last
year's leaves, I cannot find

that alarum of hooves flying
over, the sky's tawny flash,
the thunder of ideas crashing.

Measuring the Moon

(1956)

After I read in our *Weekly Reader*
that the man-in-the-moon has no light
of his own and the hugeness of his balloon

face rising from the river is an illusion,
I slipped out of the house next evening
with a nickel to hold aloft for context

at arm's length as he hissed and melted
toward night's ceiling. Sure enough,
he didn't actually diminish from horizon

to overhead. As witnessed with my coin,
all measures were consistent. By next issue,
I no longer believed in plain seeing,

the alchemy of a full moon changing
sun gold to silver then shrinking,
the blindness of light, nor stars winking.

In a Dream of Standing in the Wings
of a Reality TV Show

I know the backstage secrets in this dream
of your life: How many shots it takes
to get up in the morning, how many pills
put you to bed. From my vantage point

behind the curtains, I see the wrinkles
in your butt through a gap of your hospital gown
and the flat swirl of sleep hair as you stand
before the judge of the X-ray machine.

Unlike your audience, I remember each
episode of how you came to be a flash
flood, the simple baby suffocation,
one electrical fire, twin crashes of stock

market and ash tree on your house, the rare
red spider's bite, that careen into guardrail,
the one long dive into the Ashtabula
after the letter from Uncle Sam about your son.

Out

Paperwhites leaning through fences
shine just as white as other
flowers behind narrow pickets.

Pooch at a back door
barks as the moon
bounces down lane bricks.

His small voice escapes
through window glass
like the dream of a child

who wants out to play,
but doesn't know desire and moonlight
are too sudden to dream him back.

In My Town: West Virginia

There's a cluster of box houses, two streetlights, a one-room post office, and a stop sign
that circle like wagons against the outside world, each familiar as the items
of a bedside table in the *kumbayah* of self-protection.

Each house has local-color shutters that stutter a chorus in wind, the same small porches
that support two pots of geraniums as if an ordinance were passed some years ago
against mums; a curious cabbage garden infects each backyard.

Two streetlights work always, except in very high winds; until 2001, we had only one.
The R&R track splits the town like a slash through a theta. Each of us as teen spent hours
out there with a friend, maybe two, listening to the dying rail hum of distant places.

Our post office has the wood from the pilothouse of a riverboat lodged there so long
in water the tiny town accrued around it. If our village's growth were a cancer,
the patient would never die.

Mail slots in the post office wear everyone's first name, except Ricky Morris's and Ricki
Lewis's. Their boxes have the ♂ and ♀ signs for last names, the postmaster's
acknowledgment that gender similarities exist.

The stop sign at the town limits stands its red watch. The last thing everyone sees
before leaving warns to look both ways and watch as the road opens up mountain
that's no longer outside our town. It has just begun the eternity of being gone.

Epiphany in a Spring Field

The small green sward, size of a front yard,
across B Street from the Stewart's Drive-in
in my little river town, has a complexion
of spring grass and sprung daisies with evening
sun sliding along, distant hills, pale green,
sparse, like a first beard. Despite four cars
and a Jolly Pirate Donuts shop
obscuring continuity of the land,
I imagine a torch from a campfire,
in my hand waving light at the fresh valley's
verbless details. Evening glowing,
endless sea of mountains fading off,
the heavy breathing of unbroken trees
beneath a salted sky, open and free.
Then red light turns green.

Visible Songs of Appalachia

1.

The certainty each morning, along the slope,
hand-holding my way among rumoring beeches,

that every second is a new thing I'm learning,
like the safe end of the buckeye;

and that awful awareness the worm-crammed
crabapple in my hand was once a young heart.

2.

Walking the hush in the buildup
of maple and sycamore leaves, the fawn-

camouflage of afternoon sun speckles,
hand-sized spans of heat between boulders,

the sense everywhere of a woman bathing.

3.

Hollow crunching of the mare
chewing corn in the barn,

her smile of froth caught in flashlight beam.
The sense that she just missed being human.

Séance

(June, 1959)

Sitting out on the back steps at night,
I whistled for dogs I did not have.
At fourteen, those times waiting
under the stars were best.

When a night bird fluttered to a tree,
a bat swooped after a mosquito
that was after me, I kept whistling,
with never a "Here, Boy"

or "Come on, Fella," just short
repetitions of the same shrill streams
of air between teeth and lips,
as if my one fiercest

work was understood only
by sharp, distant ears.
Nothing ever showed up
in the yard, but sometimes I heard

claws and whines against the back gate
and was afraid to walk to the alley.
But once I did, slowly, and heard
panting between boards

and smelled wet fur.
I looked over the top of the fence.
You were crouched there.
By your one bloodshot eye in moon-

light and both of your trembling arms,
I knew all the unspeakable things
we would soon do to each other.

Washing Seven Plates

Hands in hot foam awakening into steam,
I play with forces that shaped the world.

As they cool and dry, all seven dinner plates
lean in the rack like a mountain range of china.

My favorite cup slips into the empty basin,
shattering in discrete shapes, like fallen climbers.

In a mood from cleaning up cup shards,
I go to my primitive cellar, a match burning

and look for a file to sharpen mower blades.
When the fire in my hand dies,

just before panic, I think how my seconds
evaporate the same in dark underground

as in bright kitchen, allowing me time to do
what's next. I should get used to another cup.

Night Without Dream,
Morning Without Memory

Every now and then, when the last train plays
its harmonica to the other side

of the hills, and no more faucet drops land
on enamel, no clear crack of loose floorboards

or knee joint popping through the screen door,
I sleep without troubling phantoms.

Now and then, full of sleep, for a lifetime,
my dead out of complaints about my life, I wake

with the assured memory of nothing.
The back porch hammock I dream on melts

like early fog, and I float, swimming karma
back down to zero. These times are the same,

apex of one gable, obverse of the single
coin, self-same moment of emptied sleep,

filled wakefulness, one second in the center
of the merry-go-round, tigers melting.

Gravitas

The lumber of one leg
against the other, minutes
in an eon of sleeping.

The weight of pain
in the heavenward gaze
the tormented have
with their rising.

The long name of burden
in one hand pressing against
an ankle swelling,
the provenance of standing.

All the bones, old as motion
collecting in the ache before the step.

Sleeping Among Horses

We dreamt of running, our manes singing
all the songs the wind knew.
When you rolled over,

your hand slapped me like a mare's tail;
I woke with grass in my mouth.
Two horses sniffed toward us a pace.

Their eyes wide as black moons,
they froze smelling whether
we were wolves. Once they sniffed

two groggy campers and went
back to mating, we were no more
to them than flies.

Between

In my dreams, you're always in a hurry,
looking for our friend who's long gone
from our waking. Your shirt buttoned

crooked, your hair lying back at an odd
angle, you look as if you've just awakened,
too, from searching for him who has slipped

away somewhere. But most disturbing,
now that you are also gone, is that I am
out on the street between buildings trying

to surmise which way you might have taken off—
whether it is the same as his going. I feel,
looking each way down shining bricks,

that barbershop-mirror effect: The afternoon
we sat in our sheets, in three chairs,
waving both ways at endless reflections.

The Dead

I'll be one. You'll be one.
For now, we have such

ceremonies of growing old
to come: I put one tired hand

around yours on the teacup.
Together we dream of cooling.

Summer Solstice Prayer, 2008

Like a dollop of butter melting
in an iron skillet, the full moon sizzles
across the sky.
      There's plenty of nature
still to worship. And I do,
watching pipistrelles flutter
like handkerchiefs at hungry mosquitoes.
      Tonight,
all seem to work toward the height of the heavens.
As if it's the desire of nature to lift us there
by vision.
      And in this river valley
awash in light, something new—
but so old I scarcely notice—
      recalls me
to the sheen of blood, whether my own
or that of the smashed insect on my arm.

Lone Dogs

And the truth is both dog and wolf are ancient . . .
—BRIGIT PEGEEN KELLY

They come in ones and twos each winter,
trotting hard across hillsides and ranging
through pastures. No hand sets down
regular bowls of scraps soaked in bacon grease.

They come transformed from the coveting
of house or barn, believing in forest again,
to conjure the family curse of hunting
that hovers, like the moon at midday, pale,

bone-colored. Snow lies on the woolly bodies
of half-eaten sheep and cold rings
invisible axes in the woods. I sit here
gray evenings on hillsides, each January

turning myself again into what I must be
to wait for each collarless dog appearing
in my crosshairs, and, next day, lift
into the wagon each stiff, wolfish body.

Laughter Fossils

First, we mined every stratum,
going down and back with our
little shovels and our brushes.

Then, we dug with every tool lighter
than a back-hoe, breaking into tomb
and smashing into antechamber

finding little more than
if we'd sat out among dunes,
drinking martinis and watching

sand chisel away the sunset.
We searched every era,
and with wrong tools, uncovered

only the hilarity of Tuscan bowls,
the buffoonery of Belgian oubliettes.
But of laughter turned solid,

or preserved in a balloon beside
the mouth of one tribesman or trilobite,
we discovered nothing, no hard grins,

no stone guffaws, as if in all
history, laughter never owns—
only rents the air.

Camel in the Rainforest, Giraffe in the Rockies

Their spans of throat remain
out of easy reach of plains lion
or field tiger, one suited for the dry
expanse of dunes, the other
for the highest leaves of savanna trees.

In the Amazon
the camel cannot lope—
his humps swelling or deflating
like balloons with the one thing
he's not had to cope—heavy rains.
He staggers in undergrowth,
legs a tangle in thick vines.

The giraffe lost on slopes
and cliffs—his legs cross,
confused as beach chairs
in high wind—could easily
tumble to his death—
gatefold table flying
from a skyscraper into depths.

I should have let them stay
as they were, as evolution has.
Time leaden on my hands,
I flipped through
my daughter's animal stories
beside her in recovery.

The Way the World Goes On

The sun claws the river all day
as if to keep it swelling as we sleep,

evening vines relax, giving up
heat they've stored since noon, the breeze

changes, painted grass points the way
it escaped, and the moon watches

expressionless waters gurgle down
our streets as if searching for a flood;

while each thing that is one thing continues
its work on becoming another,

like leaves toward black compost under trees,
a wick stutters out in the pool of wax

that was its candle and no one
sees the end of radiance or the curtain

over the window on the gray alley
giving up its borrowed light.

Every Day of the Dead

An old church house abandoned long enough
has constantly dark windows. Two
tree limbs stretch across
its walk—like the arms of one who fell
long ago. Back garden vines vein
over a skeletal trellis.

A cemetery of leaning stones
cools before and after rain. Fence corners
overgrown with blue-gray, even on sunny days,
are harder to remember at night.
Shadows of shadows on humps of earth,
portals—we come to touch
the world we may believe in,

as the long-gone may come to a ray
of evening sun against a mausoleum wall,
for the memory
of memory and warmth
of body we think they must believe in.

Crossing

Here's the fall day with all
the pain each moment can bring,
the interminable freight train

at the rutted crossing,
the day in which every second
seems pitted against human will,

where the bridge has iced
at rush hour and everyone's
slewing out of line.

Even on this bright day, bars
of sun spell out defiance.
Every pathway must be blocked

by construction for us to know
the way home. The temperature
has steadily to drop. Cats fight

through the hours for one windless
spot on the porch. Then the stove must
tick all night against the clock.

We need all the fretting we can get
to remind us what we're resisting
next morning when clear snow falls.

Hymn to Her

Around the parlor, her five cats
sit calm as Buddhas. Here she

dwells, at home only at home.
Outside the tedious crumble

of brick walls, she becomes
other. Outside her windows,

spring is becoming its scruffy
self: I see the flicker

worrying the spruce bark
for its beetle and the black hole

at the center of the galaxy
in the same light—even though

I am not there to catch either—
as I see her, her cats, her

universe with a sense
of the solitude of each sight.

Dream of Two Fields in Evening Rain

Boulders may not hum,
or limbs bend brushing themselves
where dust has hung;

grass cannot lean toward last light
where clouds rubbed
the sun away.

But birds wait in trees,
their eyes on me as I approach
the open center.

When a late flock rushes over,
only my shoulders quicken.
Small gems

on grass and stem won't wink as rain
increases.
Beneath the sod of two fields,

directions change:
fetid leaves,
many earthworms, coiled snails,

too far apart to count, a knot of roots
and twigs past
untying, layers of the old dreams.

A train hugs itself up hill.
Rain takes all night,
gliding, one field to the other.

Winter Cellar

December, pale crickets
sang of coming snow.
The risen river seeped
among cracks separating
concrete into a gray ice flow.

When the temperature above
dropped to ten,
I went down to turn off
the water valve, but also, despite
how it sounds, to visit them.

Against one damp wall,
they clung
like believers gathered
to pray. I thought one
or two would've sung.

At the dead bottom
of most winters,
young and old gone
from the wall, I put my ear
close by a few survivors.

Trapped in frozen pipes,
their last moans
for summer, echoes
in hardened water, live
now only as stone.

Your Christmas Present

(after Dave Smith)

This year your present to me is the memory
of the time power went out. You left your
cold coffee and your office at school
to put the note on my truck window
telling me to stop by your apartment for tickles

and hugs. A giant transformer, somewhere
in West Virginia burnt: Electricity off
the next four days till Christmas. And the sky
came back each night. Stars like Van Gogh's
bruised the dark. Your neighbor,

the valetudinarian called it the End Times.
She kept shouting from her kitchen,
"We should have known it would be on
a Christmas." You took her six candles,
she calmed down. Tinting your hair

by stove light in the kitchen that evening,
you cried when it turned the color
of blood. We played with everything
not electrical. We baked donuts, wound
several old clocks, colored-in

newspaper cartoons by flickering light,
promising each other it couldn't get better.
Tying the red ribbon just now on a box
for you, I opened your present again.

In a Park, a Crow in Spring Rain

He sits along a spruce bough
like an exclamation of the winter
we just made it through.

His emphasis on black,
he seems bereft, a placeholder,
marking some lack,

the negative space about
the only green that lived
the winter. I just

give him too much power,
like a wizard scanning
the world from his tower

for the word or seed that might
unmake spring,
allow winter night

to blossom again. I've drunk
too much, sat here long
on the hood of my truck.

Kids and moms settle
back onto swings and slides;
reborn sun heats the metal.

I need to lie down, become a park
bench that upholds both sun
and snow with disregard.

I look rain slick, I know,
too starkly wet, planning
the murder of one crow.

Wind on the River

When young, I was never convinced how
terrible old age would be, any more than
I was the river flowed west under waves

wrinkling east. Now, the trick of the aged
seems, with ineffectual speech, to have been
half-persuading us of time's terror.

Old people's words were distant lights
in night windows, bright, highly visible,
but giving neither vision nor direction.

Of late, I have a crazy hunger for bread
to toss to catfish in the river.
I only ever wanted to pull them out before.

Minimum

1.

In my town, a cluster of houses,
two streetlights, a one-room post office,
and a stop sign whisper that this is
a -ville, a -burg, a -ton.

2.

At the capital museum's "Indian Village"
diorama, no moccasined foot ever trod
its grass-plugged plain, not one war whoop
ever rattled clouds. None of the soldiers
see, but they all stare.

3.

The tiny cemetery the other side
of my neighbor has one piece of wrought iron
fencing its corner, a lichen-covered
and cracked headstone dated 1789,
and another lying in grass with half

the date and name worn away.
If a single item here sank, disappeared,
or was stolen by vandals, its somber
identity would crumble.

4.

The fewest snowflakes to keep a blizzard
trapped in a glass globe that rests
on my grandmother's bed table—
just enough snow to make it
seem endless when I pick it up.

Let alone, the naked air stays clear.
The church with doors that don't open,
windows that won't raise, just stands.
A glassy sky waits. The least
snow sleeps on everything.

Young Scientist Learning Soft

At sunset, I cannot let the soft things go.
They bang their heads into the porch light
they pray to, to let them in. Nothing
lessens the panic of brown crickets

leaping from cellar walls. Their home
lost in a light-flood, they could question
first their abandonment to night. I know
the world as mostly fire and fright.

It pulses in the flesh of each hand
I shake. I know it flicking the jarfly's
plastic wing. I know it towing her into air
on twine. The green skin of the katydid

flexes and rises to meet match fire.
In this light, everything must marry
and writhe, turning into ghosts of smoke.
Hard-shelled things curl to death in sleep.

Out the window, the staff of breeze carries
less and less the hymns of autumn.
It will not be over until everything is one.
I bite my licorice and watch the fun.

In Mythic Times

(1966)

Somewhere, I believed,
my life had once been better than at this school.
Somewhere no one noticed what kind of word
I ended my sentences with.
It only mattered that I began.

Walking down the halls, I suspected
others of knowing what I'd been through.
That some clipped their hair like mine
was no accident. That I'd stood on a high balcony
in a black uniform trimmed

in ermine, and that crowds had known
my name and named their firstborn
after me. And everyone believed I'd
found Nibelung treasures or Melungeon bones,
reburying them for better days.

I'd step out, someday, ragged
and bloody, in everyone's behalf
from the mountainside with the great fleece
and goat's horn. Old mothers and maiden
aunts, even witches curling in their bowers,

forgetting the first syllable
they heard of magic, remember my name
whispered over them as infants
lest they come, like so many others
from our school, to nothing.

The Lion That Finds You
Asleep in His Dream

(after Rousseau's *The Sleeping Gypsy*)

Under shadow of stars,
lost in dust-light of moon,
he pads the distance to where you
should not be, where trees

are too far apart to hear any sounds.
He pads up hissing the song
you hum before sleep.

From his throat of castanets,
he rattles his hunger,
whiskers against your ear.

Never mind river, never mind rainbow,
his tail points the way he came
from a mound of bones
once a person asleep on sand.

The moon's still high in its arc,
and you know
you spilled from this lion's heart.